Contents

Corn on the Cob with Garlic Herb Butter

    4   to 5 ears of corn, husked
  1/2   cup (1 stick) unsalted butter, softened
    3   to 4 cloves garlic, minced
    2   tablespoons minced fresh Italian parsley
        Salt and black pepper
    2   cups water

1. Place each ear of corn on a piece of foil. Combine butter, garlic and parsley in small bowl; spread onto corn. Season with salt and pepper; tightly seal foil.

2. Place in **CROCK-POT®** slow cooker, overlapping ears, if necessary. Add water. Cover; cook on LOW 4 to 5 hours or on HIGH 2 to 2 1/2 hours.

Makes 4 to 5 servings

Cod Tapenade

> **4** **cod fillets or other firm white fish (2 to 3 pounds total)**
> **Salt and black pepper**
> **2** **lemons, thinly sliced**
> **Tapenade (recipe follows)**

1. Season cod with salt and pepper. Arrange half of lemon slices in bottom of **CROCK-POT®** slow cooker. Top with cod; cover with remaining lemon slices.

2. Cover; cook on HIGH 1 hour or until fish is just cooked through. Prepare Tapenade. Remove fish to serving plates; discard lemon. Top with Tapenade.

Makes 4 servings

Tapenade

> **¹/₂** **pound pitted kalamata olives**
> **2** **tablespoons chopped fresh thyme or Italian parsley**
> **2** **tablespoons capers, drained**
> **2** **tablespoons anchovy paste**
> **1** **clove garlic**
> **¹/₄** **teaspoon grated orange peel**
> **¹/₈** **teaspoon ground red pepper**
> **¹/₂** **cup olive oil**

Place olives, thyme, capers, anchovy paste, garlic, orange peel and ground red pepper in food processor or blender; pulse to roughly chop. Add oil; pulse briefly to form a chunky paste.

Makes about 1 cup

Confetti Black Beans

1	cup dried black beans
3	cups water
1½	teaspoons olive oil
1	medium onion, chopped
¼	cup chopped red bell pepper
¼	cup chopped yellow bell pepper
1	jalapeño pepper, finely chopped*
1	large tomato, seeded and chopped
½	teaspoon salt
⅛	teaspoon black pepper
2	cloves garlic, minced
1	can (about 14 ounces) chicken broth
1	whole bay leaf

Jalapeño peppers can sting and irritate the skin, so wear rubber gloves when handling peppers and do not touch your eyes.

1. Rinse and sort beans; cover with water. Soak 8 hours or overnight.** Drain.

2. Heat oil in large skillet over medium heat. Add onion, bell peppers and jalapeño pepper; cook and stir 5 minutes or until onion is tender. Add tomato, salt and black pepper; cook 5 minutes. Stir in garlic.

3. Place beans, broth and bay leaf in **CROCK-POT**® slow cooker. Add onion mixture. Cover; cook on LOW 7 to 8 hours or on HIGH 4½ to 5 hours or until beans are tender. Remove and discard bay leaf.

Makes 6 servings

**To quick soak beans, place beans in large saucepan; cover with water. Bring to a boil over high heat. Boil 2 minutes. Remove from heat; let soak, covered, 1 hour.

Fruit Ambrosia with Dumplings

- **4 cups fresh or frozen fruit (strawberries, raspberries or peaches)**
- **$1/2$ cup plus 2 tablespoons granulated sugar, divided**
- **$1/2$ cup warm apple or cran-apple juice**
- **2 tablespoons quick-cooking tapioca**
- **1 cup all-purpose flour**
- **$1^1/4$ teaspoons baking powder**
- **$1/4$ teaspoon salt**
- **3 tablespoons butter or margarine, cut into small pieces**
- **$1/2$ cup milk**
- **1 egg**
- **2 tablespoons packed light brown sugar, plus additional for garnish**

1. Combine fruit, $1/2$ cup granulated sugar, juice and tapioca in **CROCK-POT®** slow cooker. Cover; cook on LOW 5 to 6 hours or on HIGH $2^1/2$ to 3 hours or until sauce thickens.

2. Combine flour, 2 tablespoons granulated sugar, baking powder and salt in medium bowl. Cut in butter using pastry cutter or two knives until mixture resembles coarse crumbs. Whisk milk and egg in small bowl. Pour milk mixture into flour mixture. Stir until soft dough forms.

3. Drop dough by teaspoonfuls on top of fruit. Sprinkle with 2 tablespoons brown sugar. Cover; cook on HIGH 30 minutes to 1 hour or until toothpick inserted into centers of dumplings comes out clean.

4. Serve warm. Sprinkle dumplings with additional brown sugar, if desired.

Makes 4 to 6 servings

Spicy Beans Tex-Mex

- $1/3$ **cup lentils**
- $1^1/3$ **cups water**
- 5 **slices bacon**
- 1 **onion, chopped**
- 1 **can (about 15 ounces) pinto beans, rinsed and drained**
- 1 **can (about 15 ounces) red kidney beans, rinsed and drained**
- 1 **can (about 14 ounces) diced tomatoes**
- 3 **tablespoons ketchup**
- 3 **cloves garlic, minced**
- 1 **teaspoon chili powder**
- $1/2$ **teaspoon ground cumin**
- $1/4$ **teaspoon red pepper flakes**
- 1 **whole bay leaf**

1. Combine lentils and water in large saucepan. Bring to a boil over medium-high heat. Boil 20 to 30 minutes; drain.

2. Heat large skillet over medium heat. Add bacon; cook and stir until crisp. Remove to paper towel-lined plate; crumble when cool enough to handle. Add onion to same skillet; cook and stir 5 minutes or until tender.

3. Combine lentils, bacon, onion, beans, tomatoes, ketchup, garlic, chili powder, cumin, red pepper flakes and bay leaf in **CROCK-POT®** slow cooker. Cover; cook on LOW 5 to 6 hours or on HIGH 3 to 4 hours. Remove and discard bay leaf.

Makes 8 to 10 servings

Steamed Southern Sweet Potato Custard

- **1 can (16 ounces) cut sweet potatoes, drained**
- **1 can (12 ounces) evaporated milk, divided**
- **$1/2$ cup packed brown sugar**
- **2 eggs, lightly beaten**
- **1 teaspoon ground cinnamon**
- **$1/2$ teaspoon ground ginger**
- **$1/4$ teaspoon salt**
- **Whipped cream (optional)**
- **Ground nutmeg (optional)**

1. Place sweet potatoes and $1/4$ cup evaporated milk in food processor or blender; process until smooth. Add remaining evaporated milk, brown sugar, eggs, cinnamon, ginger and salt; process until well blended. Pour into ungreased 1-quart soufflé dish. Cover tightly with foil. Crumple large sheet (15×12 inches) of foil; place in bottom of **CROCK-POT®** slow cooker. Pour 2 cups water over foil. Make foil handles. (See Note.)

2. Remove dish to **CROCK-POT®** slow cooker over foil handles. Cover; cook on HIGH $2^1/2$ to 3 hours or until skewer inserted into center comes out clean.

3. Use foil handles to remove dish to wire rack. Uncover; let stand 30 minutes. Garnish with whipped cream and nutmeg.

Makes 4 servings

Note: To make foil handles, tear off three 18×3-inch strips of heavy-duty foil or use regular foil folded to double thickness. Crisscross strips in spoke design and place in **CROCK-POT®** slow cooker to make lifting dish easier.

Quinoa and Vegetable Medley

2 medium sweet potatoes, cut into $1/2$-inch-thick slices
1 medium eggplant, cut into $1/2$-inch cubes
1 large green bell pepper, sliced
1 medium tomato, cut into wedges
1 small onion, cut into wedges
$1/2$ teaspoon salt
$1/4$ teaspoon ground red pepper
$1/4$ teaspoon black pepper
1 cup uncooked quinoa
2 cups vegetable broth
2 cloves garlic, minced
$1/2$ teaspoon dried thyme
$1/4$ teaspoon dried marjoram

1. Coat inside of **CROCK-POT®** slow cooker with nonstick cooking spray. Combine sweet potatoes, eggplant, bell pepper, tomato, onion, salt, ground red pepper and black pepper in **CROCK-POT®** slow cooker; toss to coat.

2. Place quinoa in strainer; rinse well. Add quinoa to vegetable mixture in **CROCK-POT®** slow cooker. Stir in broth, garlic, thyme and marjoram. Cover; cook on LOW 5 hours or on HIGH $2^{1}/2$ hours or until quinoa is tender and broth is absorbed.

Makes 6 servings

Risotto-Style Peppered Rice

- 1 **can (about 14 ounces) vegetable broth**
- 1 **cup uncooked converted long grain rice**
- 1 **medium green bell pepper, chopped**
- 1 **medium red bell pepper, chopped**
- 1 **cup chopped onion**
- ¹/₂ **teaspoon ground turmeric**
- ¹/₈ **teaspoon ground red pepper (optional)**
- 4 **ounces Monterey Jack cheese with jalapeño peppers, cubed**
- 1 **cup (1 stick) butter, cut into small pieces**
- ¹/₂ **cup milk**
- 1 **teaspoon salt**

1. Combine broth, rice, bell peppers, onion, turmeric and ground red pepper, if desired, in **CROCK-POT®** slow cooker; stir to blend. Cover; cook on LOW 4 to 5 hours or until rice is tender and broth is absorbed.

2. Stir in cheese, butter, milk and salt; fluff rice with fork. Cover; cook on LOW 5 minutes or until cheese melts.

Makes 4 to 6 servings

Tip: Dairy products should be added at the end of the cooking time, because they will curdle if cooked in the **CROCK-POT®** slow cooker for a long time.

Pear Crunch

           1 **can (8 ounces) crushed pineapple in juice, undrained**
        $1/4$ **cup pineapple or apple juice**
           3 **tablespoons dried cranberries**
       $1^1/2$ **teaspoons quick-cooking tapioca**
        $1/4$ **teaspoon vanilla**
           2 **pears, cored and halved**
        $1/4$ **cup granola with almonds**
             Sprigs fresh mint (optional)

1. Combine pineapple, pineapple juice, cranberries, tapioca and vanilla in **CROCK-POT®** slow cooker; stir to blend. Top with pears, cut sides down.

2. Cover; cook on LOW $3^1/2$ to $4^1/2$ hours. Arrange pear halves on serving plates. Spoon pineapple mixture over pears. Sprinkle with granola. Garnish with mint.

Makes 4 servings

Spiced Apple Tea

- **3 bags cinnamon herbal tea**
- **3 cups boiling water**
- **2 cups unsweetened apple juice**
- **6 whole cloves**
- **1 cinnamon stick**

1. Place tea bags in **CROCK-POT®** slow cooker. Pour boiling water over tea bags; cover and let stand 10 minutes. Remove and discard tea bags.

2. Add apple juice, cloves and cinnamon stick to **CROCK-POT®** slow cooker. Cover; cook on LOW 2 to 3 hours. Remove and discard cloves and cinnamon stick. Serve warm in mugs.

Makes 4 servings

Lemon and Tangerine Glazed Carrots

- **6 cups sliced carrots**
- **1¹/₂ cups apple juice**
- **6 tablespoons butter**
- **¹/₄ cup packed brown sugar**
- **2 tablespoons grated lemon peel**
- **2 tablespoons grated tangerine peel**
- **¹/₂ teaspoon salt**
- **Chopped fresh Italian parsley (optional)**

Combine carrots, apple juice, butter, brown sugar, lemon peel, tangerine peel and salt in **CROCK-POT®** slow cooker; stir to blend. Cover; cook on LOW 4 to 5 hours or on HIGH 1 to 3 hours. Garnish with parsley.

Makes 10 to 12 servings

Spiced Apple Tea

Barley Salad

- **2 onions, chopped**
- **2 sweet potatoes, diced**
- **1 cup pearl barley**
- **1 teaspoon salt**
- **¹/₂ teaspoon cinnamon**
- **¹/₄ teaspoon ground red pepper (optional)**
- **1¹/₂ cups water**
- **2 apples, peeled and chopped**
- **1 cup dried cranberries**
- **1 cup chopped pecans**

1. Spread onions and sweet potatoes in bottom of **CROCK-POT®** slow cooker. Add barley, salt, cinnamon and ground red pepper, if desired. Pour in water.

2. Cover; cook on LOW 4 hours or on HIGH 2 hours. Stir in apples, cranberries and pecans.

Makes 16 servings

Onion Marmalade

- **1 bottle (12 ounces) balsamic vinegar**
- **1 bottle (12 ounces) white wine vinegar**
- **2 tablespoons water**
- **3 tablespoons arrowroot or cornstarch**
- **1 1/2 cups packed dark brown sugar**
- **2 teaspoons cumin seeds**
- **2 teaspoons coriander seeds**
- **4 large yellow onions, halved and thinly sliced**

1. With exhaust fan running, cook vinegars in large saucepan over high heat until reduced to $1/4$ cup. Sauce will be thick and syrupy. Remove from heat. Stir water into arrowroot in small bowl until smooth. Add brown sugar, cumin, coriander and arrowroot mixture to sauce; blend well.

2. Place onions in **CROCK-POT®** slow cooker. Stir in vinegar mixture. Cover; cook on LOW 8 to 10 hours or HIGH 4 to 6 hours, stirring occasionally. Store in refrigerator up to two weeks.

Makes 5 cups

Tip: Serve as a side dish or condiment with eggs, roasted vegetables, meats or on sandwiches.

Milk and Honey Corn Pudding

1	**package (3 ounces) cream cheese**
2	**cans (about 15 ounces *each*) cream-style corn**
1	**can (16 ounces) corn**
1	**package (8¹/₂ ounces) corn muffin mix**
1	**cup evaporated milk**
3	**eggs**
¹/₃	**cup honey**
2	**tablespoons butter, cut into small pieces**
1	**teaspoon salt**

1. Coat inside of **CROCK-POT®** slow cooker with nonstick cooking spray. Place cream cheese in large microwavable bowl. Microwave 30 seconds on HIGH or until melted. Add corn, muffin mix, evaporated milk, eggs, honey, butter and salt; stir until butter is melted and mixture is creamy.

2. Pour batter into **CROCK-POT®** slow cooker. Cover, cook on LOW 4¹/₂ hours or until pudding is golden and knife inserted into the center comes out clean. Turn off heat. Let rest 10 minutes before serving.

Makes 8 servings

Sauvignon Blanc Beef with Beets and Thyme

- 1 pound red or yellow beets, scrubbed and quartered
- 2 tablespoons extra virgin olive oil
- 1 boneless beef chuck roast (about 3 pounds)*
- 1 medium yellow onion, peeled and quartered
- 2 cloves garlic, minced
- 5 sprigs fresh thyme
- 1 whole bay leaf
- 2 whole cloves
- 1 cup chicken broth
- 1 cup Sauvignon Blanc or dry white wine
- 2 tablespoons tomato paste
- Salt and black pepper

*Unless you have a 5-, 6- or 7-quart CROCK-POT® slow cooker, cut any roast larger than 2¹/₂ pounds in half so it cooks completely.

1. Layer beets evenly in **CROCK-POT®** slow cooker.

2. Heat oil in large skillet over medium heat. Add roast; cook 4 to 5 minutes or until browned on all sides. Add onion and garlic during last few minutes of browning. Remove to **CROCK-POT®** slow cooker.

3. Add thyme, bay leaf and cloves to **CROCK-POT®** slow cooker. Combine broth, wine, tomato paste, salt and pepper in medium bowl; stir to blend. Pour over roast and beets in **CROCK-POT®** slow cooker. Cover; cook on LOW 8 to 10 hours. Remove and discard bay leaf.

Makes 6 servings

Sausage and Swiss Chard Stuffed Mushrooms

- 1/2 **pound bulk pork sausage**
- 1/2 **onion, finely chopped**
- 2 **cups chopped Swiss chard**
- 1/4 **teaspoon dried thyme**
- 2 **tablespoons garlic-and-herb-flavored dried bread crumbs**
- 1 1/2 **cups chicken broth, divided**
- 1/2 **teaspoon salt, divided**
- 1/2 **teaspoon black pepper, divided**
- 2 **packages (6 ounces *each*) cremini mushrooms, stemmed***
- 3 **tablespoons olive oil, divided**
- 2 **tablespoons grated Parmesan cheese**
- 2 **tablespoons chopped fresh Italian parsley**

Do not substitute with white button mushrooms.

1. Coat inside of **CROCK-POT®** slow cooker with nonstick cooking spray. Heat medium skillet over medium heat. Add sausage; cook and stir 6 to 8 minutes or until browned. Remove sausage to medium bowl using slotted spoon.

2. Add onion to skillet; cook and stir 3 minutes or until translucent, scraping up any browned bits from bottom of skillet. Stir in chard and thyme; cook 1 to 2 minutes or until chard is wilted. Remove from heat.

3. Stir in sausage, bread crumbs, 1 tablespoon broth, 1/4 teaspoon salt and 1/4 teaspoon pepper. Brush oil over mushrooms. Season with remaining 1/4 teaspoon salt and 1/4 teaspoon pepper. Fill mushrooms evenly with stuffing.

4. Pour remaining broth into **CROCK-POT®** slow cooker. Arrange stuffed mushrooms in bottom. Cover; cook on HIGH 3 hours. To serve, remove mushrooms using slotted spoon; discard cooking liquid. Combine cheese and parsley in small bowl; sprinkle evenly over mushrooms.

Makes 6 to 8 servings

Chicken Liver Pâté

Pâté

1¹/₂ **pounds chicken livers, trimmed of fat and membrane**

1 **small onion, thinly sliced**

3 **sprigs fresh thyme**

2 **cloves garlic, crushed**

¹/₄ **teaspoon salt**

1 **tablespoon water**

3 **tablespoons cold butter, cut into 4 pieces**

2 **tablespoons whipping cream**

2 **tablespoons dry sherry**

Topping

¹/₂ **shallot, minced**

2 **tablespoons chopped fresh parsley**

1 **tablespoon sherry vinegar**

¹/₈ **teaspoon sugar**

Salt and black pepper

Assorted crackers or Melba toast

1. For Pâté, rinse chicken livers; pat dry. Place in **CROCK-POT®** slow cooker. Add onion, thyme, garlic, salt and water. Cover; cook on LOW 2 hours.

2. Remove and discard thyme sprigs. Pour remaining ingredients from **CROCK-POT®** slow cooker into strainer; cool.

3. Remove to food processor or blender; pulse to coarsely chop livers. Add butter, one piece at a time, pulsing after each addition just to combine. Add whipping cream and sherry; pulse to combine. Remove to serving bowl. Cover; refrigerate 3 hours or until firm.

4. For Topping, stir together shallot, parsley, vinegar, sugar, salt and pepper in small bowl. Set aside 5 minutes, then spoon over pâté. Serve with crackers.

Makes 8 to 10 servings

Finer Fare

Steamed Artichokes

> **4**   **artichokes, trimmed and cut in half**
>
> **Juice of $1/2$ lemon**
>
> **Tarragon Browned Butter Dipping Sauce (recipe follows), Cream Cheese-Bacon Dipping Sauce (recipe follows) and/or Garlic-Herb Butter Dipping Sauce (page 35)**

Place trimmed artichokes cut side down in bottom of **CROCK-POT®** slow cooker. Add enough water to come halfway up artichokes; add lemon juice. Cover; cook on LOW 6 hours. Prepare and serve with Dipping Sauce(s).

Makes 8 servings

Tarragon Browned Butter Dipping Sauce

> **1**   **cup (2 sticks) butter**
>
> **4**   **teaspoons dried tarragon *or* $1/4$ cup finely chopped fresh tarragon**

Melt butter in medium saucepan over medium heat. Cook, swirling butter in saucepan over heat until butter is light brown. Remove from heat; stir in tarragon. Pour into **CROCK-POT® LITTLE DIPPER®** slow cooker. Cover to serve warm.

Makes about 1 cup

Cream Cheese-Bacon Dipping Sauce

> **4**   **ounces cream cheese**
>
> **1**   **cup whipping cream**
>
> **$1/2$**   **teaspoon black pepper**
>
> **8**   **slices bacon, crisp-cooked and finely chopped**

Whisk cream cheese and whipping cream in medium saucepan over medium heat until smooth. Stir in pepper and bacon. Pour into **CROCK-POT® LITTLE DIPPER®** slow cooker. Cover to serve warm.

Makes about 1 cup

Garlic-Herb Butter Dipping Sauce

- **1 cup (2 sticks) butter**
- **8 cloves garlic, crushed**
- **$1/2$ cup chopped fresh herbs such as Italian parsley or chives**

Melt butter in medium saucepan over medium heat. Add garlic; cook and stir until garlic is golden brown. Remove from heat. Strain garlic from sauce; stir in herbs. Pour into **CROCK-POT® LITTLE DIPPER®** slow cooker; cover to keep warm.

Makes about 1 cup

Shrimp and Pepper Bisque

- **1 can (about 14 ounces) chicken broth**
- **1 bag (12 ounces) frozen bell pepper stir-fry mix, thawed**
- **1/2 pound frozen cauliflower florets**
- **1 stalk celery, sliced**
- **1 tablespoon seafood seasoning**
- **1/2 teaspoon dried thyme**
- **12 ounces medium raw shrimp, peeled and deveined**
- **2 cups half-and-half**
- **2 to 3 green onions, finely chopped**

1. Combine broth, stir-fry mix, cauliflower, celery, seafood seasoning and thyme in **CROCK-POT®** slow cooker; stir to blend. Cover; cook on LOW 8 hours or on HIGH 4 hours.

2. Stir in shrimp. Cover; cook on HIGH 15 minutes or until shrimp are pink and opaque. Add soup in batches to blender or food processor; pureé. Return to **CROCK-POT®** slow cooker. Stir in half-and-half. Ladle into bowls and sprinkle with green onions.

Makes 4 servings

Tip: For a creamier, smoother consistency, strain through several layers of damp cheesecloth.

Stuffed Baby Bell Peppers

- **1 tablespoon olive oil**
- **1/2 onion, chopped**
- **1/2 pound ground beef, chicken or turkey**
- **1/2 cup cooked rice**
- **3 tablespoons chopped fresh Italian parsley**
- **2 tablespoons lemon juice**
- **1 tablespoon dried dill weed**
- **1 tablespoon tomato paste, divided**
- **1/2 teaspoon salt**
- **1/8 teaspoon black pepper**
- **1/4 cup beef or chicken broth**
- **1 bag yellow and red baby bell peppers (about 2 dozen)**

1. Heat oil in medium skillet over medium heat. Add onion; cook and stir 5 minutes or until translucent.

2. Add beef; brown 6 to 8 minutes, stirring to break up meat. Remove to large bowl, using slotted spoon. Add rice, parsley, lemon juice, dill weed, 1 1/2 teaspoons tomato paste, salt and black pepper; mix well. Whisk broth and remaining 1 1/2 teaspoons tomato paste in small bowl.

3. Cut lengthwise slit down side of each bell pepper; run under cold water to wash out seeds. Fill each bell pepper with 2 to 3 teaspoons meat mixture. Place filled bell peppers in **CROCK-POT®** slow cooker, filling side up. Add broth mixture. Cover; cook on LOW 5 hours or on HIGH 2 1/2 hours.

Makes 16 to 18 servings

Chicken Tagine with Lemon and Olives

1	onion, finely chopped
4	cloves garlic, minced
	Grated peel and juice of 1 lemon
2	tablespoons chopped fresh rosemary *or* 2 teaspoons dried rosemary
1	tablespoon fresh thyme *or* 1 teaspoon dried thyme
4	chicken leg quarters
20	pitted green olives, crushed
2	tablespoons butter, cut into small pieces
2	tablespoons water
2	tablespoons all-purpose flour

1. Combine onion, garlic, lemon peel and juice, rosemary and thyme in **CROCK-POT®** slow cooker; stir to blend. Top with chicken, olives and butter. Cover; cook on LOW 5 to 6 hours.

2. Remove chicken. Turn **CROCK-POT®** slow cooker to HIGH. Stir water into flour in small bowl; whisk into **CROCK-POT®** slow cooker. Cover; cook on HIGH 15 minutes or until sauce is thickened.

Makes 4 servings

Saffron-Scented Shrimp Paella

3 tablespoons olive oil, divided

1¹⁄₂ cups chopped onions

4 cloves garlic, thinly sliced

   Salt

1 cup roasted red bell pepper, diced

1 cup chopped tomato

1 whole bay leaf

1 large pinch saffron

1 cup dry white wine

8 cups chicken broth

4 cups uncooked rice

25 large raw shrimp, peeled and deveined (with tails on)

   White pepper

1. Heat 2 tablespoons oil in large skillet over medium heat. Add onions, garlic and salt; cook and stir 5 minutes or until translucent. Add bell pepper, tomato, bay leaf and saffron; cook and stir until heated through. Add wine. Continue cooking until liquid is reduced by half. Add broth. Bring to a simmer. Adjust seasonings, if desired, and stir in rice. Remove to **CROCK-POT®** slow cooker. Cover; cook on HIGH 30 minutes to 1 hour or until liquid is absorbed.

2. Toss shrimp in remaining 1 tablespoon oil in large bowl. Season with salt and white pepper. Place shrimp on rice in **CROCK-POT®** slow cooker. Cover; cook on HIGH 10 minutes or until shrimp are pink and opaque. Remove and discard bay leaf.

Makes 4 to 6 servings

Simmered Napa Cabbage with Dried Apricots

- **4** cups napa cabbage or green cabbage, cored, cleaned and thinly sliced
- **1** cup chopped dried apricots
- **¹⁄₄** cup clover honey
- **2** tablespoons orange juice
- **¹⁄₂** cup dry red wine
  Salt and black pepper
  Grated orange peel (optional)

1. Combine cabbage and apricots in **CROCK-POT®** slow cooker; toss well. Combine honey and orange juice in small bowl; stir until smooth. Drizzle over cabbage. Add wine.

2. Cover; cook on LOW 5 to 6 hours or on HIGH 2 to 3 hours or until cabbage is tender. Season with salt and pepper. Garnish with orange peel.

Makes 4 servings

Spicy Thai Coconut Soup

- **3** cups coarsely shredded cooked chicken (about 12 ounces)
- **2** cups chicken broth
- **1** can (15 ounces) straw mushrooms, drained
- **1** can (13$^1/_2$ ounces) unsweetened coconut milk
- **1** can (about 8 ounces) baby corn, drained
- **1** tablespoon minced fresh ginger
- **$^1/_2$** to 1 teaspoon red curry paste*
- **2** tablespoons lime juice
- **$^1/_4$** cup chopped fresh cilantro

Red curry paste can be found in jars in the Asian food section of large grocery stores. Spice levels can vary between brands. Start with $^1/_2$ teaspoon, then add more as desired.

Combine chicken, broth, mushrooms, coconut milk, corn, ginger and curry paste in **CROCK-POT®** slow cooker; stir to blend. Cover; cook on HIGH 2 to 3 hours. Stir in lime juice and sprinkle with cilantro just before serving.

Makes 4 servings

Ham and Sage Stuffed Cornish Hens

- 1 **cup plus 3 tablespoons sliced celery, divided**
- 1 **cup sliced leek (white part only)**
- 2 **tablespoons butter, divided**
- $1/4$ **cup finely diced onion**
- $1/4$ **cup diced smoked ham or prosciutto**
- 1 **cup seasoned stuffing mix**
- 1 **cup chicken broth**
- 1 **tablespoon finely chopped fresh sage** *or* 1 **teaspoon ground sage**
- 4 **Cornish hens (about $1^{1}/2$ pounds** *each***)**
  Salt and black pepper

1. Coat inside of **CROCK-POT®** slow cooker with nonstick cooking spray. Combine 1 cup celery and leek in **CROCK-POT®** slow cooker.

2. Melt 1 tablespoon butter in large skillet over medium heat. Add remaining 3 tablespoons celery, onion and ham; cook and stir 5 minutes or until onion is soft. Stir in stuffing mix, broth and sage. Remove mixture to medium bowl.

3. Rinse hens and pat dry. Sprinkle inside and outside of each hen with salt and pepper. Gently spoon stuffing into cavities. Tie each hen's drumsticks together with kitchen string.

4. Melt remaining 1 tablespoon butter in same skillet over medium-high heat. Place 2 hens, breast sides down, in skillet; cook until skins brown, turning to brown all sides. Remove to **CROCK-POT®** slow cooker. Repeat with remaining hens. Cover; cook on LOW 5 to 6 hours or on HIGH 3 to 4 hours. Remove string; place hens on large serving platter. Spoon cooking broth over hens.

Makes 4 servings

Braised Sea Bass with Aromatic Vegetables

- **2 tablespoons butter or olive oil**
- **2 bulbs fennel, thinly sliced**
- **3 large carrots, julienned**
- **3 large leeks, thinly sliced**
  Salt and black pepper
- **6 fillets sea bass or other firm-fleshed white fish (2 to 3 pounds total)**

1. Melt butter in large skillet over medium-high heat. Add fennel, carrots and leeks; cook and stir until beginning to soften and lightly brown. Season with salt and pepper. Arrange half of vegetables in bottom of **CROCK-POT®** slow cooker.

2. Season bass with salt and pepper; place on top of vegetables in **CROCK-POT®** slow cooker. Top with remaining vegetables. Cover; cook on LOW 2 to 3 hours or on HIGH 1 to $1\frac{1}{2}$ hours or until fish is cooked through.

Makes 6 servings

Wild Rice and Dried Cherry Risotto

- 1 **cup dry-roasted salted peanuts**
- 6 **teaspoons sesame oil, divided**
- 1 **cup chopped onion**
- 6 **ounces uncooked wild rice**
- 1 **cup diced carrots**
- 1 **cup chopped green or red bell pepper**
- $^1/_2$ **cup dried cherries**
- $^1/_8$ **to $^1/_4$ teaspoon red pepper flakes**
- 4 **cups hot water**
- $^1/_4$ **cup teriyaki or soy sauce**
- 1 **teaspoon salt**

1. Coat inside of **CROCK-POT®** slow cooker with nonstick cooking spray. Heat large skillet over medium-high heat. Add peanuts; cook and stir 2 to 3 minutes or until nuts begin to brown. Remove nuts to plate; set aside.

2. Heat 2 teaspoons oil in skillet. Add onion; cook and stir 6 minutes or until browned. Remove to **CROCK-POT®** slow cooker.

3. Stir in rice, carrots, bell pepper, cherries, red pepper flakes and water. Cover; cook on HIGH 3 hours.

4. Turn off heat. Let stand 15 minutes, uncovered, until rice absorbs liquid. Stir in teriyaki sauce, peanuts, remaining 4 teaspoons oil and salt.

Makes 8 to 10 servings

Ham with Fruited Bourbon Sauce

- 1 **bone-in ham (about 6 pounds)**
- $^1/_2$ **cup apple juice**
- $^3/_4$ **cup packed dark brown sugar**
- $^1/_2$ **cup raisins**
- 1 **teaspoon ground cinnamon**
- $^1/_4$ **teaspoon red pepper flakes**
- $^1/_3$ **cup dried cherries**
- $^1/_4$ **cup bourbon, rum or apple juice**
- $^1/_4$ **cup cornstarch**

1. Coat inside of **CROCK-POT®** slow cooker with nonstick cooking spray. Add ham (cut side down), apple juice, brown sugar, raisins, cinnamon and red pepper flakes. Cover; cook on LOW 9 to 10 hours or on HIGH $4^1/_2$ to 5 hours. Add cherries 30 minutes before end of cooking time.

2. Turn off heat. Remove ham to large cutting board. Cover loosely with foil; let stand 10 to 15 minutes before slicing.

3. Let cooking liquid stand 5 minutes. Skim off and discard fat. Turn **CROCK-POT®** slow cooker to HIGH. Stir bourbon into cornstarch in small bowl until smooth; whisk into cooking liquid. Cover; cook on HIGH 10 to 15 minutes or until sauce is thickened. Serve sauce over ham.

Makes 10 to 12 servings

Tip: Spraying the inside of the **CROCK-POT®** slow cooker with nonstick cooking spray before adding the ingredients makes cleanup much easier.

Corn Bread Stuffing with Sausage and Green Apples

1   package (16 ounces) honey corn bread mix, plus ingredients to prepare mix

2   cups cubed French bread

1¹/₂   pounds mild Italian sausage, casings removed

1   onion, finely chopped

1   green apple, peeled, cored and diced

2   stalks celery, finely chopped

¹/₂   teaspoon salt

¹/₄   teaspoon dried sage

¹/₄   teaspoon dried rosemary

¹/₄   teaspoon dried thyme

¹/₄   teaspoon black pepper

3   cups chicken broth

2   tablespoons chopped fresh Italian parsley (optional)

1. Mix and bake corn bread according to package directions. Cool; cover with plastic wrap and set aside overnight.*

2. Coat inside of **CROCK-POT®** slow cooker with nonstick cooking spray. Preheat oven to 350°F. Cut corn bread into 1-inch cubes. Spread corn bread and French bread on large baking sheet. Toast in oven 20 minutes or until dry.

3. Brown sausage in medium skillet over medium-high heat 6 to 8 minutes, stirring to break up meat. Remove sausage to **CROCK-POT®** slow cooker using slotted spoon.

4. Add onion, apple and celery to skillet; cook and stir 5 minutes or until softened. Stir in salt, sage, rosemary, thyme and pepper. Remove mixture to **CROCK-POT®** slow cooker.

5. Add bread cubes; stir gently to combine. Pour broth over mixture. Cover; cook on HIGH 3 to 3¹/₂ hours or until liquid is absorbed. Garnish with parsley.

Or purchase prepared 8-inch square pan of corn bread. Proceed as directed.

Makes 8 to 12 servings

Tip: Consider using your **CROCK-POT®** slow cooker as an extra "oven" or "burner" for holiday entertaining. For example, the **CROCK-POT®** slow cooker can cook the stuffing while the holiday turkey is in the oven.

Buttery Vegetable Gratin

- 3 **leeks, halved lengthwise and cut into 1-inch pieces**
- 1 **red bell pepper, cut into $^1/_2$-inch pieces**
- 5 **tablespoons unsalted butter, cubed and divided**
- 4 **tablespoons grated Parmesan cheese, divided**
- 1 **teaspoon fresh thyme, divided**
- $^3/_4$ **teaspoon salt, divided**
- $^1/_4$ **plus $^1/_8$ teaspoon black pepper, divided**
- 2 **zucchini (about $1^1/_2$ pounds total), cut into $^3/_4$-inch-thick slices**
- 2 **yellow squash (about $1^1/_2$ pounds total), cut into $^3/_4$-inch-thick slices**
- $1^1/_2$ **cups fresh bread crumbs**

1. Coat inside of **CROCK-POT®** slow cooker with nonstick cooking spray. Place leeks and bell pepper in bottom of **CROCK-POT®** slow cooker. Dot with 1 tablespoon butter, 1 tablespoon cheese, $^1/_2$ teaspoon thyme, $^1/_4$ teaspoon salt and $^1/_8$ teaspoon black pepper.

2. Arrange zucchini in single layer over leeks, overlapping as necessary. Dot with 1 tablespoon butter, 1 tablespoon cheese, remaining $^1/_2$ teaspoon thyme, $^1/_4$ teaspoon salt and $^1/_8$ teaspoon black pepper.

3. Arrange yellow squash in single layer over zucchini, overlapping as necessary. Dot with 1 tablespoon butter, remaining 2 tablespoons cheese, $^1/_4$ teaspoon salt and $^1/_8$ teaspoon black pepper. Cover; cook on LOW 4 to 5 hours or until vegetables are soft.

4. Meanwhile, melt remaining 2 tablespoons butter in large skillet over medium-high heat. Add bread crumbs; cook and stir 6 minutes or until crisp and golden brown. Remove to medium bowl; set aside to cool. Sprinkle over vegetable mixture just before serving.

Makes 12 servings

Beef Stew with Molasses and Raisins

2	pounds cubed beef stew meat
1/3	cup all-purpose flour
2	teaspoons salt, divided
1 1/2	teaspoons black pepper, divided
5	tablespoons oil, divided
2	medium onions, sliced
1	can (28 ounces) diced tomatoes, drained
1	cup beef broth
3	tablespoons molasses
2	tablespoons cider vinegar
4	cloves garlic, minced
2	teaspoons dried thyme
1	teaspoon celery salt
1	whole bay leaf
8	ounces baby carrots, cut in half lengthwise
2	parsnips, diced
1/2	cup golden raisins

1. Combine beef, flour, 1 1/2 teaspoons salt and 1 teaspoon pepper in large bowl; toss to coat meat. Heat 2 tablespoons oil in large skillet or Dutch oven over medium-high heat. Brown beef in two batches, adding additional 2 tablespoons oil as needed.

2. Add remaining 1 tablespoon oil to skillet. Add onions; cook 5 minutes, stirring to scrape up any browned bits. Add tomatoes, broth, molasses, vinegar, garlic, thyme, celery salt, bay leaf and remaining 1/2 teaspoon salt and 1/2 teaspoon pepper. Bring to a boil. Add beef; boil 1 minute.

3. Remove mixture to **CROCK-POT®** slow cooker. Cover; cook on LOW 5 hours or on HIGH 2$^{1}/_{2}$ hours. Add carrots, parsnips and raisins. Cover; cook on LOW 1 to 2 hours or until vegetables are tender. Remove and discard bay leaf.

Makes 6 to 8 servings

Sweet Potato and Pecan Casserole

- **1 can (40 ounces) sweet potatoes, drained and mashed**
- **$1/2$ cup apple juice**
- **$1/3$ cup plus 2 tablespoons butter, melted and divided**
- **$1/2$ teaspoon salt**
- **$1/2$ teaspoon ground cinnamon**
- **$1/4$ teaspoon black pepper**
- **2 eggs, beaten**
- **$1/3$ cup chopped pecans**
- **$1/3$ cup packed brown sugar**
- **2 tablespoons all-purpose flour**

1. Combine potatoes, apple juice, $1/3$ cup butter, salt, cinnamon and pepper in large bowl; beat in eggs. Pour mixture into **CROCK-POT®** slow cooker.

2. Combine pecans, brown sugar, flour and remaining 2 tablespoons butter in small bowl; stir to blend. Spread over sweet potatoes. Cover; cook on HIGH 3 to 4 hours.

Makes 6 to 8 servings

Roast Ham with Tangy Mustard Glaze

- **1 fully-cooked boneless ham (about 3 pounds), trimmed**
- **¹/₄ cup packed dark brown sugar**
- **2 tablespoons lemon juice, divided**
- **1 tablespoon Dijon mustard**
- **¹/₂ teaspoon ground allspice**
- **¹/₄ cup granulated sugar**
- **2 tablespoons cornstarch**

1. Place ham in **CROCK-POT®** slow cooker. Combine brown sugar, 2 teaspoons lemon juice, mustard and allspice in small bowl; stir to blend. Spoon evenly over ham. Cover; cook on LOW 6 to 7 hours or until ham is heated through. Remove ham to large warm serving platter. Cover loosely with foil.

2. Turn **CROCK-POT®** slow cooker to HIGH. Add granulated sugar, cornstarch and remaining 4 teaspoons lemon juice to cooking liquid. Cover; cook on HIGH 10 to 15 minutes or until sauce is thickened. Carve ham into slices and spoon sauce evenly over individual servings.

Makes 12 to 15 servings

Autumn Herbed Chicken with Fennel and Squash

   3 **to 4 pounds chicken thighs**
      Salt and black pepper
      All-purpose flour
   2 **tablespoons olive oil**
   1 **fennel bulb, thinly sliced**
 $^1/_2$ **butternut squash, seeded and cut into $^3/_4$-inch cubes**
   1 **teaspoon dried thyme**
 $^1/_2$ **cup walnuts**
 $^1/_2$ **cup chicken broth**
 $^1/_2$ **cup apple cider or juice**
      Hot cooked rice
 $^1/_4$ **cup fresh basil, sliced into ribbons**
   2 **teaspoons fresh rosemary, finely minced**

1. Season chicken with salt and pepper; lightly coat chicken with flour. Heat oil in large skillet over medium heat. Working in batches, brown chicken 3 to 5 minutes on each side. Remove to **CROCK-POT®** slow cooker using slotted spoon.

2. Stir fennel, squash and thyme into **CROCK-POT®** slow cooker until combined. Add walnuts, broth and cider to **CROCK-POT®** slow cooker. Cover; cook on LOW 5 to 7 hours or on HIGH $2^1/_2$ to $4^1/_2$ hours. Serve over rice. Garnish with basil and rosemary.

Makes 6 servings

Brussels Sprouts with Bacon, Thyme and Raisins

2 **pounds Brussels sprouts**
1 **cup chicken broth**
²/₃ **cup golden raisins**
2 **thick slices applewood smoked bacon, chopped**
2 **tablespoons chopped fresh thyme**

Trim ends from sprouts; cut in half lengthwise through core (or in quarters). Combine Brussels sprouts, broth, raisins, bacon and thyme in **CROCK-POT®** slow cooker. Cover; cook on LOW 3 to 4 hours.

Makes 8 servings

Harvest Ham Supper

6 **carrots, cut into 2-inch pieces**
3 **medium sweet potatoes, quartered**
1 **to 1¹/₂ pounds boneless ham**
1 **cup maple syrup**

Arrange carrots and sweet potatoes in bottom of **CROCK-POT®** slow cooker. Place ham on top of vegetables. Pour syrup over ham and vegetables. Cover; cook on LOW 6 to 8 hours.

Makes 6 servings

Brussels Sprouts with
Bacon, Thyme and Raisins

Green Bean Casserole

- **2 packages (10 ounces *each*) frozen green beans**
- **1 can (10³/₄ ounces) condensed cream of mushroom soup, undiluted**
- **1 tablespoon chopped fresh Italian parsley**
- **1 tablespoon chopped roasted red peppers**
- **1 teaspoon dried sage**
- **¹/₂ teaspoon salt**
- **¹/₂ teaspoon black pepper**
- **¹/₄ teaspoon ground nutmeg**
- **¹/₂ cup toasted slivered almonds***

*To toast almonds, spread in single layer in small heavy skillet. Cook and stir over medium heat 1 to 2 minutes or until nuts are lightly browned.

Combine beans, soup, parsley, red peppers, sage, salt, black pepper and nutmeg in **CROCK-POT®** slow cooker; stir to blend. Cover; cook on LOW 3 to 4 hours. Sprinkle with almonds.

Makes 6 servings

Pork Roast with Currant Cherry Salsa

- 1 1/2 **teaspoons chili powder**
- 3/4 **teaspoon salt**
- 1/2 **teaspoon garlic powder**
- 1/2 **teaspoon paprika**
- 1/4 **teaspoon ground allspice**
- 1 **boneless pork loin roast (2 pounds)**
  Nonstick cooking spray
- 1/2 **cup water**
- 1 **package (1 pound) frozen pitted dark cherries, thawed, drained and halved**
- 1/4 **cup currants or dark raisins**
- 1 **teaspoon grated orange peel**
- 1 **teaspoon balsamic vinegar**
- 1/8 **to** 1/4 **teaspoon red pepper flakes**

1. Combine chili powder, salt, garlic powder, paprika and allspice in small bowl; stir to blend. Rub roast evenly with spice mixture, pressing spices into roast.

2. Spray large skillet with cooking spray; heat over medium-high heat. Add roast; cook 6 to 8 minutes or until browned on all sides. Place in **CROCK-POT®** slow cooker.

3. Pour water into skillet, stirring to scrape up any brown bits. Pour liquid into **CROCK-POT®** slow cooker around roast. Cover; cook on LOW 6 to 8 hours.

4. Remove roast to large cutting board. Cover loosely with foil; let stand 10 to 15 minutes. Strain juices from **CROCK-POT®** slow cooker; discard solids. Pour juice into small saucepan; keep warm over low heat.

5. Turn **CROCK-POT®** slow cooker to HIGH. Add cherries, currants, orange peel, vinegar and red pepper flakes to **CROCK-POT®** slow cooker. Cover; cook on HIGH 30 minutes. Slice pork; spoon warm juices over meat. Serve with salsa.

Makes 8 servings

Horseradish Roast Beef and Potatoes

1 tablespoon minced fresh Italian parsley

1 teaspoon dried thyme, basil or oregano

1 tablespoon freshly grated horseradish

1 tablespoon Dijon mustard

3 pounds beef roast*

1 to 2 pounds Yukon Gold potatoes, quartered

1 pound mushrooms, cut into large pieces

2 cans (about 14 ounces *each*) beef broth

2 large tomatoes, seeded and diced

1 large onion, sliced

1 green bell pepper, chopped

1 red bell pepper, chopped

1 cup dry red wine

3 cloves garlic, minced

1 whole bay leaf

Salt and black pepper

Unless you have a 5-, 6- or 7-quart CROCK-POT® slow cooker, cut any roast larger than 2¹/₂ pounds in half so it cooks completely.

1. Combine parsley, thyme, horseradish and mustard in small bowl to make a paste. Place roast in **CROCK-POT®** slow cooker; spread paste over roast.

2. Add potatoes, mushrooms, broth, tomatoes, onion, bell peppers, wine, garlic, bay leaf, salt and black pepper to **CROCK-POT®** slow cooker; stir to blend. Add enough water to cover roast and vegetables. Cover; cook on HIGH 2 hours. Turn **CROCK-POT®** slow cooker to LOW. Cover; cook on LOW 4 to 6 hours. Remove and discard bay leaf.

Makes 12 servings

Pumpkin Bread Pudding

- **2 cups milk**
- **1/2 cup (1 stick) plus 2 tablespoons butter, divided**
- **1 cup packed brown sugar, divided**
- **1 cup solid-pack pumpkin**
- **3 eggs**
- **1 tablespoon ground cinnamon**
- **2 teaspoons vanilla**
- **1/2 teaspoon ground nutmeg**
- **1/4 teaspoon salt**
- **16 slices cinnamon raisin bread, torn into small pieces (8 cups total)**
- **1/2 cup whipping cream**

1. Combine milk and 2 tablespoons butter in medium microwavable bowl. Microwave on HIGH 2 1/2 to 3 minutes.

2. Whisk 1/2 cup brown sugar, pumpkin, eggs, cinnamon, vanilla, nutmeg and salt in large bowl until well blended. Whisk in milk mixture until blended. Add bread cubes; toss to coat.

3. Coat inside of **CROCK-POT®** slow cooker with nonstick cooking spray. Remove bread mixture to **CROCK-POT®** slow cooker. Cover; cook on HIGH 2 hours or until knife inserted in center comes out clean. Turn off heat. Uncover; let stand 15 minutes.

4. Combine remaining 1/2 cup butter, remaining 1/2 cup brown sugar and whipping cream in small saucepan; bring to a boil over high heat, stirring frequently. Remove from heat. Spoon bread pudding into individual bowls; top with sauce.

Makes 8 servings

Beef with Apples and Sweet Potatoes

- **1 boneless beef chuck shoulder roast (about 2 pounds), trimmed and cut into 2-inch cubes**
- **1 can (40 ounces) sweet potatoes, drained**
- **2 small onions, sliced**
- **2 apples, peeled, cored and sliced**
- **¹/₂ cup beef broth**
- **2 cloves garlic, minced**
- **1 teaspoon salt**
- **1 teaspoon dried thyme, divided**
- **³/₄ teaspoon black pepper, divided**
- **2 tablespoons cold water**
- **1 tablespoon cornstarch**
- **¹/₄ teaspoon ground cinnamon**

1. Place beef, sweet potatoes, onions, apples, broth, garlic, salt, ¹/₂ teaspoon thyme and ¹/₂ teaspoon pepper in **CROCK-POT®** slow cooker. Cover; cook on LOW 8 to 9 hours.

2. Remove beef, sweet potatoes, onions and apples to large bowl; cover with foil to keep warm. Turn off heat. Let cooking liquid stand 5 minutes. Skim off fat and discard.

3. Stir water into cornstarch, remaining ¹/₂ teaspoon thyme, ¹/₄ teaspoon pepper and cinnamon in small bowl until smooth; whisk into cooking liquid. Turn **CROCK-POT®** slow cooker to HIGH. Cover; cook on HIGH 15 minutes or until cooking liquid is thickened. Serve sauce over beef mixture.

Makes 6 servings

Index